THE SECRETARY OF THE NAVY

I0426372

SECNAV M-5213.1
DECEMBER 2005

DEPARTMENT OF THE NAVY

FORMS MANAGEMENT MANUAL

PUBLISHED BY
THE DEPARTMENT OF THE NAVY CHIEF INFORMATION OFFICER

DEPARTMENT OF THE NAVY

OFFICE OF THE CHIEF INFORMATION OFFICER
1000 NAVY PENTAGON
WASHINGTON, DC 20350-1000

31 December 2005

FOREWORD

This manual implements the policy set forth in Secretary of the Navy Instruction (SECNAVINST) 5210.16, *Department of the Navy (DON) Forms Management and Information Requirements (Reports) Management Programs*, 31 December 2005 regarding forms management and is issued under the authority of SECNAVINST 5430.7N, *Assignment of Responsibilities and Authorities in the Office of the Secretary of the Navy*, 9 June 2005. SECNAVINST 5213.10D, *Department of the Navy (DON) Forms Management Program*, 24 December 1992 was cancelled by separate administrative action.

This Manual specifies procedures for forms management within the Department of the Navy. Effective forms management ensures that the number of forms utilized by the Department is minimized and that those in use are effective, efficient, and economical.

This Manual is effective immediately; it is mandatory and applicable to the Offices of the Secretary of the Navy, The Chief of Naval Operations (CNO), the Commandant of the Marine Corps (CMC), and all Navy and Marine Corps activities, installations, commands, ships, and stations.

This manual may be accessed through the Department of the Navy, Navy Electronic Directives System website: http://neds.daps.dla.mil/. For further assistance or to offer comments and recommendation concerning this manual, contact the offices delineated below:

Office of the Secretary
and Navy Forms Manager
(CNO/DNS-5)
720 Kennon St. SE
Bldg 36 Room 203
Washington DC 20374
Commercial: (202) 433-2835
DSN: 288-2835

Marine Corps Forms Manager
(ARDE)
HQMC
2 Navy Annex
Washington DC 20380-1775

Commercial: (703) 614-1712
DSN: 224-1712

D. M. Wennergren
Department of the Navy
Chief Information Officer

Department Of The Navy
Forms Management Manual

TABLE OF CONTENTS

FIGURES

REFERENCES

(a) Title 44 United States Code (USC), Chapters 21, 25, 27, 29, 31, and 33

(b) Title 44 USC Chapter 35, "Paperwork Reduction Act of 1995" as amended

(c) Title 5 USC Chapter 5 § 552a, "Records Maintained on Individuals"

(g) Section 508 of the Rehabilitation Act of 1973 as amended (29 USC 794d)

(f) Title 41 Federal Management Regulations (FMR) Part 102-193, "Creation, Maintenance, and Use of Records"

(g) Title 41 FMR Part 102-194, "Standard and Optional Forms Management Program"

(e) Title 5 Code of Federal Regulations (CFR) Part 1320, "Controlling Paperwork Burdens of the Public"

(k) DOD 5400.11-R, "Department of Defense Privacy Program," August 31, 1983, authorized by DODD 5400.11, "DOD Privacy Program," November 16, 2004

(l) DOD 7750.7-M, "DOD Forms Management Program Procedures Manual," August 1991, authorized by DODI 7750.7, "DOD Forms Management Program," May 31, 1990

(h) SECNAVINST 5211.5D, "Department of Navy Privacy Act (PA) Program," 17 July 1992

(k) SECNAVINST 5510.36, "DON Information Security Program (ISP) Regulations," 17 March 1999

(l) OPNAVINST 5218.7B, "Navy Official Mail Management Instructions," 21 October 1998

(i) SECNAV Manual M-5210.1, "Department of the Navy Records Management Manual," 31 December 2005

(j) SECNAV Manual M-5210.2, "Department of the Navy Standard Subject Identification Code (SSIC) Manual," 31 December 2005

PART I

INTRODUCTION

1. <u>Background</u>. Forms management ensures that forms provide needed information effectively, efficiently and economically. Information is vital to the success of any organization and provides the basis for management decisions. Specific types of data are needed to meet particular requirements and forms are a major means for providing a fast and easy method of collecting information. As information requirements change, effective forms management provides for improved forms and control of the proliferation of authorized forms. In turn, this minimizes the burden of DON forms and maximizes their effectiveness.

PART II

FORMS MANAGEMENT

1. Forms Management. Forms management consists of:

a. Analysis and control: The development or improvement of data elements and forms design on proposed or existing forms and the review and coordination of forms to ensure efficient response to management requirements.

b. Printing and stocking: The decision-making process of determining how the form is to be stocked and distributed. The forms manager must know how to stock forms in the supply system, how to write printing specifications, and how to aid the form's sponsor in determining the amount of forms to be stocked.

c. Web based, electronically fillable forms, often provide potential cost and time burden savings when compared to traditional paper forms and "print and fill" forms available on the Intranet.

2. Analysis and Control.

a. Forms must be constructed to obtain all needed information concisely, economically, and effectively. Instructions for completing a form, if needed, should be sufficiently clear to avoid misinterpretation.

b. Each item on the form must be necessary to satisfy a current need or known future requirement. Creating a form to meet some possible future need is not justified.

c. The need for a form can be determined by analyzing the answers to the following questions:

(1) Is the information required under the cognizance of the originating office?

(2) Is all the information requested necessary?

(3) How will the information be used?

(4) Can the information be obtained from another source?

(5) Is the request for information clearly stated?

d. Each data item on the form must be arranged in logical format for easy completion by the preparing organization and for efficient use by the receiving organization.

e. Determine the organization that can furnish precise,

usable information in the easiest way. Reassignment of the responsibility for preparation of forms may avoid establishment of duplicate source records, unnecessary workflow, or other uneconomical processes.

    f. Distribution of completed forms is based on a "need-to-know" basis. Do not distribute courtesy copies.

    g. Costing

        (1) <u>Need for Costing</u>. Consider the cost of establishing new forms and in improving existing forms. Compare investment of work-hours and other costs to the value received from the form. Effective decision-making processes, in some cases, justify costly forms. Depending on the circumstances, web based, electronically fillable forms, may provide lower costs.

        (2) <u>Methods of Estimating Costs</u>. Base estimates on the actual situation. Estimate work hours and machine time from the approximate time spent by command personnel to prepare and process the form. Obtain dollar costs of any machine time, printing, special equipment, or other materials from the command completing the form.

    h. The required method of control is the assignment of a form number by the forms manager. This number enables the forms manager to track each form from development to cancellation.

3. <u>Printing and Stocking</u>.

    a. Forms will be printed by the Document Automated and Production Service (DAPS) and will be stocked and available for order at Navy Forms Online, http://forms.daps.dla.mil. Local reproduction of any type will not be authorized for forms that are available. Forms managers may authorize local reproduction if DON-wide use is fewer than 100 forms annually.

    b. The sponsor is responsible for providing information for obtaining the forms. Forms used within a designated office, such as routing slips with codes or names, do not require accompanying written document. Forms used by personnel outside the designated office must be included in a requiring document, usually an instruction, notice, order to inform potential users that the forms exist. This information is located in the last paragraph of the requiring document (above the signature) and contains the form number, revision date, title, stock number, and other ordering information, if applicable.

    c. Actual copies of forms will not be included in the requiring document unless a sample is specifically needed to aid the respondents in completing the form. If an unusual circumstance requires that a blank copy of the form be included in the directive for a specific reason, the word "SAMPLE" must be overlaid (e.g. through a watermark) on the form to prevent unauthorized reproduction of the form.

4. <u>Excess Stock</u>. The Navy Forms Online website (http://forms.daps.dla.mil) is the central stocking point for all forms, has the authority to dispose of excess stock of any form that has not been ordered during a 2 year timeframe, upon approval from the forms manager.

5. <u>Beneficial Suggestions</u>.

    a. Suggestions for improvements to SFs or OFs are to be forwarded to the suggestor's forms manager. Since these forms are used government-wide and have no DON sponsor, the suggestion, with individual endorsements as to why the suggestion should be approved, must be forwarded through the chain of command to the SECNAV/OPNAV Forms Manager. DON commands or activities within this chain of command have the authority to disapprove the suggestion. If the appropriate service forms manager concurs with the suggestion and individual endorsements, the suggestion will be provided to OSD/WHS for review and, if appropriate, forwarded to GSA for final action.

    b. Suggestions for improvements to DD forms are to be provided to the navy or Marine Corps sponsor of the DD form for comments. If the suggestion has merit it can be forwarded, with comments and concurrences, to the OPNAV/SECNAV Forms Manager for review and, if appropriate, forwarding to OSD/WHS for final action.

Figure-1. Forms Precedence

General Services Administration Used by all Government agencies.	Standard Form (SF) Optional Form (OF)
Office of The Secretary Of Defense Used by DoD Staff Offices, Army, DON, and Air Force.	Department of Defense (DD) Forms
Department of the Navy Forms Established by Office of the Secretary, OPNAV and Marine Corps Headquarters	DON-wide Forms
Navy and Marine Corps Commands Established for internal use in a specific command.	Internal Forms

FIRST LEVEL FORMS -- SF/OF FORMS

Established for government-wide use. OSD and DON personnel shall not create any form that duplicates SF or OF Forms

SECOND LEVEL FORM -- DD FORMS

Established for DoD-wide use. DON personnel shall not create any form that duplicates a DD Form.

THIRD LEVEL FORM -- DON FORMS

Established for use in more than one command

FOURTH LEVEL FORM -- INTERNAL FORMS

Established for use within a specific navy/mc command

PART III

STANDARD FORMS AND OPTIONAL FORMS

1. <u>Purpose</u>. To define procedures and responsibilities for the development, clearance, and standardization of Standard Forms (SF) and Optional Forms (OF).

2. <u>Background</u>.

    a. The General Services Administration (GSA) is the central point for coordinating and controlling all SFs and OFs. GSA is also responsible for printing and stocking those forms not available on the GSA website, except for those authorized for local reproduction, those stocked by the sponsoring agency, and those few forms available only from the Superintendent of Documents, U.S. Government Printing Office http://www.gpo.gov

    b. The Office of Secretary of Defense/Washington Headquarters Services (OSD/WHS) serves as the DOD single point of contact for all matters relating to these forms. Use of Standard Forms is mandatory and if the forms available through GSA do not meet a command's needs, an exception to change or print the form in DON specifications must be obtained. Details for obtaining exceptions are contained in paragraph 7. Inquiries concerning these forms shall be submitted through the appropriate chain of command to the appropriate service forms manager.

    c. Standard and Optional Forms are the highest authority forms in the Federal Government. The Military Departments and DOD agencies must use Standard or Optional Forms whenever possible. Use of existing DD or DON forms that duplicate, even in part, Standard or Optional Forms is not authorized.

3. <u>Definitions</u>.

    a. <u>Standard Form (SF)</u>. Forms developed for use by two or more federal agencies and approved by GSA for mandatory use. The availability of these forms is generally set forth-in regulations issued by the originating agency.

    b. <u>Optional Form (OF)</u>. Forms developed for use by two or more federal agencies and approved by GSA for non-mandatory use. The availability of these forms is generally set forth-in regulations issued by the originating agency.

    c. <u>Originating Agency</u>. The federal agency, which develops a Standard or Optional Form and, after GSA approval, announces its availability for use by other federal agencies.

4. <u>Action</u>.

    a. DON personnel creating new Standard or Optional Forms shall:

(1) Ensure form is needed, information requested is essential, and does not duplicate any existing forms.

(2) Complete SF 152, Request for Clearance, Procurement, or Cancellation of Standard and Optional Forms, when a new form is proposed, an existing form is revised, or exceptions are required. Exceptions are explained in detail in paragraph 7.

(3) Provide a draft form and directive, the completed SF 152 with the justification and all coordination to the command's forms manager for review. Justification will include, but is not limited to, monetary savings, hours of personnel time saved, type of equipment used, and annual demand.

(4) Obtain written concurrences/non-concurrences of the proposed form and directive from all interested federal agencies, DOD components and military services.

(5) Notify the appropriate service forms manager in writing when forms are cancelled.

    b. The Command Forms Manager shall:

(1) Review submission to ensure that it is accurate and necessary paperwork is attached.

(2) Submit paperwork, via chain of command, to appropriate service forms manager.

(3) Maintain case folders containing necessary paperwork on forms established by the command is recommended.

    c. The SECNAV/OPNAV Forms Managers shall:

(1) Maintain official liaison with OSD/WHS on all Standard and Optional Forms matters involving the DON.

(2) Provide guidance on Standard or Optional Forms, when requested.

(3) Participate in the joint development of forms with other federal agencies and the DON organizations.

(4) Provide final review and coordination on new, revised, or canceled Standard or Optional Forms.

(5)   Provide to OSD/WHS the necessary paperwork to obtain approval of exceptions to Standard or Optional Forms.

(6)   Maintain central documentation on Standard or Optional Forms sponsored by commands.

5.   Composition of Standard or Optional Form Numbers.   These forms are written as SF 86 or OF 612 and consist of the abbreviation for Standard Form (SF) or Optional Form (OF) and the next consecutive number in the Standard Forms or Optional Forms Program.

6.   Exceptions.

a.   The following forms may be printed without GSA approval:

(1)   SFs and OFs prescribed by the Federal Acquisition Regulation (FAR) are exempt from the requirement that GSA approval be obtained prior to printing.   Under Part 53.105 of Federal Acquisition Circular 814-53, DOD users may computer generate SFs and OFs prescribed by the FAR without exception approval, providing there is no change to the content, format or sequence of the data elements and the form carries the SF or OF number and edition date.

(2)   SFs and OFs containing the statement "Local Reproduction is Authorized" may be locally printed as needed.

b.   Printing exceptions that require approval from GSA fall into the following categories:

(1)   Content exceptions changes to data elements of a form (for example, adding, deleting or changing block titles) or creating a new form instead of using an existing SF.

(2)   Format exceptions changes made by rearranging the data elements or spacing of entries on a form without changing the data elements.

(3)   Printing exceptions changes in the printing specifications because forms are not sold by GSA in constructions needed by DON.   (Most DON requests for exceptions fall in this category.)

(4) Overprinting exceptions completing blocks with repetitive information (such as an address) prior to printing. Approval is not required from GSA to overprint fill in data when blank forms are purchased from GSA stock and then overprinted in a second press run.   However, command headquarters have the

authority to approve or disapprove overprinting within their
individual commands or activities.

     c. Some exceptions may fall under more than one of the
above categories.

     d. Any exception will become invalid if the SF or OF is
revised.

7. Purchase of Negatives and Reproducibles. The Government
Printing Office (GPO) shall no longer maintain files on
negatives and reproducibles for agency exceptions to SFs. To
obtain the negatives or reproducible, submit a funded SF 1,
Printing and Binding Requisition, with the printing request.
Overprinting requires two negatives, one for the exception and
one for the overprint. Indicate on the SF 1 the number of
negatives and reproducibles needed. You must provide name,
address, and telephone of the point of contact. The negatives
must accompany each request for reprint.

8. National Stock Number. When GSA revises a form, the national
stock number does not change. Once a national stock number is
assigned to a SF or OF that number is applied to the form until
the form is cancelled. The abbreviation for the GSA stock
number is NSN (National Stock Number) and the abbreviation for
the DON stock number is S/N. GSA NSNs are not changed with
revisions; however, Navy and Marine Corps stock numbers are
changed each time a form is revised. Information concerning
Navy form stock numbers is available at
http://forms.daps.dla.mil/

PART IV

DEPARTMENT OF DEFENSE (DD) FORMS

1. Purpose. To define DON procedures and responsibilities for the development, clearance, and standardization of DD forms.

2. Background.

   a. OSD/WHS provides a central point for coordinating, controlling, designing and approving DD forms and assigning form numbers.

   b. DD forms are the highest authority forms originated in the DOD. All DON commands must use the DD forms whenever possible. Changing block headings, line spacings, deleting or adding information to a DD form or using a DON form that duplicates, even in part is not authorized.

3. Definitions.

   a. DD Form. A form used by more than one military service or DOD staff office.

   b. Prescribed DD Form. Mandatory use by all DOD components to whom the subject matter applies. Forms in this category are originated by the Secretary of Defense and prescribed by a DOD directive, instruction, or publication.

   c. Adopted DD Form. Optional use by DOD components. Forms in this category are originated by a military service or DOD staff office and implemented by a joint document or DON directive.

4. Action.

   a. Navy/Marine Corps personnel creating new DD forms shall:

      (1) Ensure form is needed, information requested is essential, and does not duplicate any existing forms.

      (2) Complete DD 67, Form Processing Action Request, when a new form is proposed, an existing form is revised, or exceptions are required. See DOD Manual 7750.7-M, August 1991, Table 2, Chapter 3 for instructions on completing DD 67.

      (3) Provide a draft form and directive, the completed DD 67 with the justification and all coordination to the command's forms manager for review. Justification will include, but is not limited to, monetary savings, hours of personnel time saved, type of equipment used, and annual demand.

(4)   Obtain written concurrences/non-concurrences of the proposed form and directive from all interested federal agencies, DOD components and military services. Commandant of the Marine Corps (ARDE) shall be included in this coordination process, if applicable.

(5)   Notify the appropriate Navy or Marine Corps forms manager, as appropriate, in writing when forms are cancelled.

b.   The Command Forms Manager shall:

(1)   Review paperwork to ensure that it is correct and all the necessary paperwork is attached.

(2)   Submit paperwork, via the chain of command, to the appropriate Navy or Marine Corps forms manager.

(3)   Maintain case folders containing necessary paperwork on forms established by the command is recommended.

c.   The Navy and Marine Corps Forms Managers shall ensure that the information on the DD 67 and the other paperwork is correct and either return the paperwork to the DON sponsor for correction or forward to the SECNAV/OPNAV Forms Manager.

d.   The SECNAV/OPNAV Forms Manager shall review the DD 67 and either return the document to the appropriate Service Forms Manager or forward OSD/WHS for approval.

5.   Composition of DD Form Numbers.   These DD form numbers are assigned by OSD/WHS. An example of a DD form number is DD 2544. DD is the abbreviation for DOD and the number 2544 is the next chronological number of the DD forms. DD form numbers shall be written as DD 2544, not DD Form 2544. This eliminates the repetition of the word "form" throughout Navy directives.

6.   Alteration.   DON personnel shall not change or modify DD forms to suit individual needs.

7.   Overprinting.   Overprinting blocks containing the same information, such as a return address block, is permissible.

8.   Printing.   DD forms may be printed in any construction (such as six-part sets, carbonless paper, etc.) unless mandatory printing specifications are provided by OSD/WHS. If there are no mandatory printing specifications, an electronic version of the form shall be provided on the DOD website http://www.dtic.mil/whs/directives/infomgt/forms/formsprogram.htm

PART V

DEPARTMENT OF NAVY FORMS

1. <u>Purpose</u>. To define procedures and responsibilities for the development, control, and use of forms required by and used within the DON.

2. <u>Procedures</u>. Each command shall provide for continuing analysis, review, and control of all forms originated or sponsored by that command to ensure that forms are effective, efficient and economical in serving their intended purpose. This includes:

     a. Reducing the paperwork burden associated with the information collection (reporting) of forms.

     b. Coordinating forms management with other records management personnel (such as reports, directives, records disposal, privacy Act) to ensure that proposed or established forms do not conflict with policies in other records management areas.

     c. Forms that may affect employees' conditions of employment shall be cleared through the DON Labor Relations Program Office, Office of Civilian Human Resources to ensure compliance with Federal labor Relations Laws.

     d. Using the minimum number of different forms necessary for the efficient and economical operation of the DON.

     e. Collecting only information on a form that is essential to accomplish a mission need.

     f. Eliminating redundant or unnecessary forms.

     g. Standardizing forms to the maximum extent practicable and consolidating lower level or duplicative forms into higher level forms using the order of precedence whenever possible.

     h. Requiring the sponsor of the form to initiate actions to create, revise, or cancel a form.

     i. Requiring that the appropriate forms manager approve the creation, revision, exception or cancellation of a form.

     j. Requiring that the electronic version of an official form be authorized by the sponsor and approved by the appropriate forms manager.

     k. Requiring that appropriate approvals and licenses for information collected from other agencies, the public or the Department of Defense be obtained and displayed on forms.

l. Preventing unauthorized disclosure of "FOR OFFICIAL USE ONLY (FOUO)" information recorded on forms by providing proper marking.

m. Using a Privacy Act Statement on forms used to collect personal information from an individual where mandated. See SECNAVINST 5211.5D.

n. Using approved DON standard data elements and codes in the design of forms.

o. Maximizing technology approved by the sponsor and forms manager to create, distribute, record, store and disseminate information entered on forms.

p. Implementing postal regulations of the United States Postal Service in forms mailing and design.

q. Ensuring forms which are created for use outside individual commands be contained in a requiring document, usually an instruction, notice, or order.

r. Reviewing all command forms annually and identifying opportunities for standardizing, eliminating duplicate or unnecessary forms, and improving the effectiveness of forms.

s. Requiring that accounting forms relating to fiscal operations are consistent with the principles, standards and related requirements prescribed by 31 U.S.C. 3511.

3. Program Objectives.

a. Increase awareness of the need for coordination with related information resources management policies and programs.

b. Ensure appropriate forms and related procedures are developed and designed to facilitate Navy/Marine Corps operations.

c. Ensure forms are cost-effective.

d. Eliminate duplication of forms through control and consolidation of those forms serving similar functions, using higher echelon forms whenever possible.

e. Ensure that DON forms approved by the command forms manager and assigned a form number shall not be changed to meet individual needs unless approval is obtained from the originator of the form and/or the person receiving the form. Forms sponsors or persons receiving the form have the authority to reject forms changed without authority.

4. Definitions.

a. Form. A fixed arrangement of captioned spaces designed

for entering and extracting prescribed information.

b. Specialty Forms. Certain printed items without fill-in spaces, such as tags, labels, and posters, may be considered as forms if they are to be stocked in the Navy supply system. These items must also be mentioned in a requiring instruction, notice, or order. Form numbers shall not be assigned to these items as matter of convenience if they are not stocked in the Navy supply system.

c. One-time Form. Developed for use for a specific project having an established termination date.

d. Test Form. Developed for testing prior to its permanent adoption. Test forms should not exceed one year.

e. Format. A guide, table, sample or exhibit that illustrates a predetermined arrangement or layout for presenting information. Most formats are largely narrative in nature and the space needed by the respondents to furnish the desired information varies substantially. Formats are often used where the arrangement and layout of items are simple and flexible and where the number of respondents is fairly limited. A format is used instead of a printed form in such instances, requiring a less expensive and more effective method of collecting the desired information. Formats should not be used in place of a standardized form or to expedite a project. Formats often place an unnecessary burden on the respondent and fail to provide the needed data.

f. Unauthorized Form. An uncontrolled form, issued without an identifying prefix or number, and not compatible with any particular method of completion. Unauthorized forms need not be completed.

g. Electronic Form. An officially proscribed set of data residing in an electronic medium with exact sequence as prescribed by the issuing component or that is used to produce a mirror-like image of the officially prescribed form. There are basically two types of electronic forms - one that is part of an automated transaction, and one where the image/data elements reside on a computer. These forms can be integrated, managed, processed, and/or transmitted through a component's information processing workflow systems.

h. Optical Character Recognition (OCR) Form. Designed for compatibility with OCR equipment which enables a machine to read by optical means human readable characters. OCR forms design is so closely related to proprietary specifications and systems requirements, forms managers should consult OCR equipment manufacturers for assistance.

i. Originator. Any command assuming responsibility for a form. The originator shall decide what items to include on the form, estimated annual usage and form availability (i.e.

stocking point or website). This information shall be submitted to the forms manager for approval. If the form will be used outside the command the originator must inform users in writing that the form is required and also provide a signed copy of the requiring instruction, notice, or order to the command's forms manager.

     j. <u>Sponsor</u>. Any command assuming responsibility for a form originated by another command or agency. An example of sponsorship is DD 2351, DOD Medical Examination Review Board, originated by the Department of the Air Force but sponsored for DON use by Chief, Bureau of Medicine and Surgery, who assumes the same responsibilities as the originator.

     k. <u>Receiver</u>. In some cases one command originates or sponsors a form but the completed form is sent to another command. In these cases, the receiving command must be part of the coordination process in order to ensure that correct information is provided.

     l. <u>Exception</u>. Form letters, formats, checklists, etc. are not considered forms and do not require form numbers unless the forms manager decides otherwise.

     m. <u>Stock Number</u>. Both GSA and DON use stock numbers to identify and order forms. Information for GSA stock numbers is contained in the "Standard and Optional Forms Facsimile Handbook" published by GSA.

5. <u>Action</u>.

     a. DON personnel creating new DON forms shall:

     (1) Ensure the form is needed. Ensure the information requested is essential and is not duplicated on any existing forms by surveying the listings of each level of forms. Initiate a DD 67.

     (2) Prepare an instruction, notice, or order to inform respondents of the existence of the form (include the requiring directive number on the form so persons receiving the form are able to match the form with the requiring directive). Office forms, i.e. forms remaining within an office, are exempt from this requirement. Obtain a Report Control Symbol if the form is part of an information collection (reporting) requirement.

     (3) Complete DD 67 to request approval.

     (4) Provide a copy of the proposed form, instruction, notice, or order with a completed DD 67 to the command's forms manager for review and approval.

(5)   Notify the command's forms manager in writing when the form is cancelled and, if necessary, remove the form from the requiring instruction, notice, or order by issuing a change transmittal or revision.

(6)   Draft a copy of the form, listing the data elements in logical order and, if needed, complete and easily understood instructions for completing the required information.

(7)   Decide how the form is to be made available, where it is to be stocked, the estimated annual demand, and the number of responses expected.

   b.   The Command Forms Manager shall:

(1)   Review the submitted documentation to ensure that it is correct.

(2)   Ensure that the form does not violate the Privacy Act of 1974 (see Chapter 1, Paragraph 2e).   Include a Privacy Act Statement (PAS) on the form, if needed.   The PAS must meet the requirements of SECNAVINST 5211.5D.   Forms containing Privacy Act Statements must be reviewed by the command's Privacy Act Official prior to approval.

(3)   Determine the fastest and easiest method to design the form.   Forms may be designed into camera-ready copy by using the Navy/Marine Corps authorized design software.   The specifications for Navy and Marine Corps forms are provided in paragraph 8 of this chapter unless the form requires mandatory printing specifications.

(4)   Assign a form number if a higher echelon number has not been assigned.

(5)   Review the proposed requiring document to ensure that all necessary information is included in the forms paragraph.   The last paragraph of the basic instruction (just above the signature line) shall include the form number, revision date, title, and the method for obtaining the form.

(6)   Provide a copy of the form to the reports manager if the form has an information collection (reporting) requirement.   If a Report Control Symbol is assigned, it must appear in the top right corner of the form immediately below the supporting directive.

(7)   Maintain an automated log of all form numbers assigned.

(8)   Maintain case folders on all current forms originated or sponsored by the command. A case folder must contain a completed DD 67, a copy of the form, the requiring directive, any other material relating to the form. When the form is cancelled, a copy of the canceling document. Form folders shall be arranged chronologically by number. (Old case folders may have an OPNAV 5213/19 in lieu of a DD 67.)

(9) Cancel all forms after notification from the originator that they are no longer required. Forward all cancelled forms containing information collection (reporting) requirements to the reports manager for appropriate action.

(10) Cancelled case folders may be destroyed or retired to Federal Records Centers by following the guidance contained in SECNAVINST 5212.5D.

6.   Composition of DON Form Numbers. An example of a DON form number is OPNAV 1000/1 (2—91) or NAVSEA 1000/1 (Rev. 2—91). A DON example from the Marine Corps is NAVMC 11023 (12-05) or MCB CLNC 1000/1 (Rev. 2-99).

a. An abbreviation for the originating command in capital letters, such as OPNAV, NAVSEA, NAVMC (Marine Corps-wide), MCB Barstow etc., or one combining the command abbreviation, usually with its location, such as NAS OCEANA. Where general forms have been developed for two or more commands within the same geographical area or chain of command, use the prefix of the Naval Supply Center stock point where the form will be stocked; for example, SAN DIEGO GEN 1000/1.

b. A standard subject identification code (SSIC), selected from SECNAV Manual M-5210.2, which best matches the title of the form. In the above example the SSIC number is 1000. NAVMC (Marine Corps-wide) forms have the SSIC located in the upper right hand corner or after edition date, i.e., NAVMC 10001 (Rev. 1-91) (1000).

c. A slash or slant (/), which separates the SSIC, number from the next consecutive number within each SSIC number. Since point numbers (or periods) are assigned to directives, dashes to Report Control Symbols, and slashes to forms, the use of the slash in the form number eliminates the need for the word "form". If the word "form" must be used it shall be placed before the command abbreviation (such as form OPNAV 1000/1 or form NAS OCEANA 1000/1).

d. The number after the slash is the next consecutive number in the SSIC series, for example, the number in the form

number OPNAV 1000/1 means this is the first form number assigned
in the 1000 SSIC series for OPNAV. Form numbers shall not
contain letters, for example OPNAV 1000/lA and OPNAV 1000/lB.
This numbering system is confusing if OPNAV 1000/IA is cancelled
and OPNAV 1000/lB remains current.

    e. The date the form is established or revised must be
included in parentheses after the form number. The date the
form is created will be shown as (2—90) and subsequent revisions
as (Rev. 4—91).

    f. The word "Test" or abbreviation "OT" (one time) after
the form number, for example, OPNAV 1000/1 (2—91) (Test) or
OPNAV 1000/1 (2—91) (OT), if applicable.

7. Design Standards. DOD design guidelines in DOD Manual
7750.7M, Chapter 4, paragraph C4.1 provide information on the
design of forms. Use the following design standards in the
preparation of Navy/Marine Corps forms, except when precluded by
special requirements or the functional use of the form:

    a. Form Size.

      (1) If printed, forms should be designed to 8-1/2 x 11
inches.

      (2) Postcard forms must measure a minimum of 3-1/2 x 5
inches, a maximum of 4-1/4 x 6 inches.

      (3) Two-page forms are not required to be printed
front and back unless required by originating/sponsoring office.

    Note: However, there are instances when designing and/or
printing forms on other than standard size paper is mandatory;
for example, some OSD/WHS and Navy/Marine Corps programs require
forms on paper larger than standard size. In these special
instances the command forms manager can authorize designing and
printing forms on other than standard size paper.

    b. Border/Margins of the Form.

      (1) Use a 1.5 point or 1/48" solid border for all four
sides, if applicable.

      (2) Unless the form has special requirements, use ½
inch page margins.

      (3) Use 1 point or 1/72" solid lines for dividing
primary sections.

      (4) Use "hairline" lines within sections.

    c. Layout of the Form.

      (1) When designing, the use of the feature "Snap to
Grid" is recommended. Grid size should be 1/10 horizontal, 1/6

vertical.

      (2) Forms are designed in box style with fillable fields having upper left captions.

      (3) Lay-out and number items in sequential order of fill-in. Numbers shall be in the upper left corner immediately before the box caption.

      (4) Group common items together on the form. Sections may be used. If several data elements pertain to the same area, individual, etc., use a section. The section title should be set flush-left margin.

      (5) National Archives and Records Administration require a separate field or block from the signature field or block for the signer's printed/typed name.

      (6) All mails or self-mailers must conform to current U. S. Postal Service regulations.

   d. Type of Font Styles for the Form.

      (1) Text fonts are Arial 8 point, or equivalent, and all Fill fonts are 10-point Times New Roman, or equivalent.

Form Part	Font Size	Letter Casing
Form Title	10 point	Upper case
Agency Disclosure Statement	8 point	Upper and lower case
Privacy Act Statement With words AUTHORITY, PRINCIPLE PURPOSE, ROUTINE USES and DISCLOSURE	8 point 8 point Bold	Upper and lower case Upper case
Section Titles	8 point Bold	Upper case
Captions	8 point	Upper case
Form Number and Edition Date	10 point Bold	Upper case
Supersession statement	8 point	Upper case

(2) Use comparable italic (optional) for words, phrases, or instructions in parentheses.

e. Title, Number, and Data of the Form.

(1) Form Title. If possible, place the title at the top or top left of the form, centered, inside the border, if applicable. Ensure the title is brief, specific, and meaningful. Eliminate any unnecessary words, such as form, label, etc. If the form does not have a standard margin, place the title, form number, and edition date in the most logical and eye-catching place.

(2) Form Number and Data. If possible, place the form number and edition date at the upper left margin, outside of the border if applicable. The form number and edition date can also be placed at the bottom, left margin also.

a. The form designation is shown in full capital letters and indicates the scope of use for the form, i.e., DON, NAVMC, command, or installation-wide. The form designation for forms used Navy-wide is "DON" or "NAVMC" for Marine Corps-wide.

b. The form designation is followed by the form number, which is assigned sequentially as new forms are created. Previously assigned form numbers are not reused.

c. The edition date consists of the month and year that the edition of the form is approved. The edition date is displayed as MM YY. Example is 04/05 immediately following the form number.

f. Supersession Notice immediately follows the edition date. Standard supersession notices used on forms include:

    PREVIOUS EDITIONS ARE OBSOLETE, or
    PREVIOUS EDITIONS WILL BE USED, or
    REPLACES (Type of Form), WHICH IS OBSOLETE.

g. Software designation. The name and producer/vendor of the software used to create the electronic form is shown in the lower right hand corner on the face page. Form users need a way to identify electronic versions of forms from printer versions, in determining the quality and accuracy of the software, and in the overall performance of the producer/vendor.

8. Classified Forms. Show appropriate security classification marking and indicate any downgrading, declassification or review

instruction as specified by SECNAVINST 5510.36 on all forms that are classified.

9. <u>Information Collection Forms</u>. In many instances forms are also requests for information and are subject to information collections (reports) control. Information collections control falls into three categories public, interagency, and internal information collections (reporting).

a. <u>Public Reporting</u>.

(1) Forms requiring information from 10 or more persons not employed by the Federal Government are considered public information collection (reporting) requirements and collection of this information must be approved by the Office of Management and Budget (OMB). Contractors employed by DON, DON dependents and retired DON personnel are considered members of the public. Forms sponsors having a form falling in this category must prepare the necessary paperwork for OMB approval and provide this information to the command's Information Collection Control Manager who shall submit the paperwork through the chain of command to the SECNAV/OPNAV forms manager who shall submit the paperwork through OSD/WHS to OMB for final approval.

NOTE: OMB notifies Congress of unauthorized public information collection (reporting) requirements and Congress then informs the agency or department that is in violation of OMB regulations to immediately take appropriate action to discontinue collecting the information.

(2) After OMB approval is obtained, the OMB control number and the expiration date (if one is assigned) of the control number must appear in the upper right corner of the form. If OMB disapproves the collection of information, the form will not be used to request information from the public.

NOTE: The OMB control number is assigned to the collection of information from the public only, not to the form itself. The expiration date, therefore, applies only to the collection of information from the public, not to the collection of information from government employees. For example, if 90 percent of the information on the form is collected from government employees and 10 percent is collected from the public, after the expiration date the action officer must discontinue collecting the information from the public but may continue collecting information from government employees, if still required.

(3) OMB approval lasts for a maximum of only three years so large quantities of stock should not be ordered if the stock will not be used by the public before the expiration date.

When the OMB approval number has expired the information cannot
be collected from the public until the forms sponsor again goes
through the approval process for an extension to continue
collecting the information.

     NOTE: If the only change to the form is the new expiration
date and large quantities of stock are still available, the old
expiration date may be crossed out and the new expiration date
added by pen.

          (4) OMB requires that an Agency Disclosure Notice
(ADN) be displayed on all forms requiring an OMB Control Number
and that the ADN be written across the form immediately below
the form title and the OMB control number. The ADN used by DOD
may be obtained from the Information Collections Control
Manager.

     b. Interagency Information Collection (Reporting). This
occurs when one department levies an information collection
requirement on another department; for example, the Department
of State may require information collection from the Departments
of Defense and Transportation. Army, Navy and Air Force are
considered part of the Department of Defense and not as separate
Departments. These information collections must be approved by
GSA and since DOD is considered the lead organization for DOD
staff offices and all Services, the Departments of Navy, Army
and Air Force do not initiate interagency information
collections but can, however, respond to interagency information
collections if tasked by DOD.

     c. Internal Information Collection (Reporting).
Information collection requirements established by and used
within DON. Additional guidance for internal information
collections (reports) is contained in SECNAV Manual M-5213.1.

PART VI

AUTOMATED FORMS

1. Authority. Title 41 Federal Management Regulations (FMR) Part 102-193, "Creation, Maintenance, and Use of Records" and Part 102-194, "Standard and Optional Forms Management Program" addresses the management of records in federal agencies, including forms management.

2. Responsibility. The head of each DON command or activity shall ensure that automated forms are created, copied, stored, transmitted, or destroyed in compliance with established policies and procedures in SECNAV Manual M-5212.1, *The Department of Navy Records Management Manual.*

3. Purpose. To provide guidelines for managing forms created, copied, stored, transmitted or destroyed by personal computers, software products, electronic data interchange, or other automated systems.

4. Definitions.

    a. Electronic Form. An officially prescribed set of data residing in an electronic medium that is used to produce a mirror-like image, or as near to mirror-like as the creation software will allow, of the officially prescribed form. An electronic form can also be one in which prescribed fields for collecting data can be integrated, managed, processed, and/or transmitted through an organization's information processing systems. There are two types of electronic forms – one that is a part of an automated transaction, such as a web-based form, and one where the image/data elements reside on a computer.

    b. Flatsheet Print on Demand Form. A form created, transmitted, and stocked electronically, but printed, filled—in, filed and stored on paper.

    c. Electronic Data Interchange (EDI). A paperless computer-to-computer exchange of routine business information. All transactions are sent and received in a machine-readable format, using nationally and internationally recognized data formats, commonly referred to as standards or transactions sets.

    d. Section 508. Section 508 of the Rehabilitation Act of 1973 as amended (29 USC 794d), requires that federal agencies' electronic and information technology is accessible to people with disabilities.

5. Background. Federal agencies rely on automated systems to create, duplicate, maintain, use and dispose of records. Many electronic records are the basis for official policy decisions and will never appear in paper format.

6. Application.

    a. The creation, maintenance, and disposition of all
official records, regardless of physical appearance, is
controlled by the provisions of 44 U.S.C. Chapters 21, 29, 31,
and 33 and National Archives and Records Administration (NARA)
regulations in 36 CFR Chapter XII Sub Chapter B.

    b. The Paperwork Reduction Act of 1995, as amended (44
U.S.C. 3501 et. seq.)calls for the coordination and integration
of Automated Data Processing (ADP), telecommunications, and
records management policies. All three of these elements are
present in automated recordkeeping systems.

    c. Forms created at any level must be Section 508
compliant. Compliance shall be based on the official Section
508 compliance criteria established in the "Electronic and
Information Technology Accessibility Standards" document
http://www.access-board.gov/sec508/guide/1194.21.htm

    d. To implement the above applications:

        (1) The Administrator of GSA is required by law to
provide guidance and assistance to federal agencies to ensure
economical and effective records management by such agencies (44
U.S.C. 2904).

        (2) The Archivist of the United States is required by
law to provide guidance and assistance to federal agencies with
respect to ensuring adequate and proper documentation of the
policies and transactions of the federal government and ensuring
proper records disposition (44 U.S.C. 3303a, 3314).

        (3) Agency heads are required to:

        (a) Make and preserve records containing
adequate and proper documentation of the organization,
functions, policies, decisions, procedures, and essential
transactions of the agency and designed to furnish the
information necessary to protect the legal and financial rights
of the government and of persons directly affected by the
agency's activities (44 U.S.C. 3101).

        (b) Submit records disposition schedules to the
Archivist of the United States for approval. No record may be
destroyed without the authorization of the Archivist (44
U.S.C.3303, 3303a, 3314).

7. <u>Action</u>.

    a. Personnel shall use the approved forms management software as directed by the Department of the Navy and accompanying policies and procedures.

    b. Personnel establishing internal forms by automated process shall ensure that the forms are submitted to the command forms manager for proper control.

    c. Personnel shall not duplicate an existing form by automated process to meet individual needs, unless given written permission from the sponsor of the form and/or command forms manager.

    d. If permission is granted to automate the form, the form shall not be altered in any way. All lines, spacing, block titles, etc must not be changed. Additions or deletions of any information is not acceptable. The originator, sponsor, or recipient of the completed form has the right to refuse to accept altered forms or forms that are submitted without permission to automate the form.

    e. Command Forms Managers shall be notified in writing of all automated forms that will be initiated, completed and/or destroyed by command personnel in accordance with SECNAV Manual M-5210.1 (*Department of the Navy Records Management Manual*)

www.ingramcontent.com/pod-product-compliance
Lightning Source LLC
Chambersburg PA
CBHW080939290526
45795CB00007BA/2818